21st Century
Basic Skills
Library

VISITING THE BEACH IN SUMMER

Published in the United States of America
by Cherry Lake Publishing
Ann Arbor, Michigan
www.cherrylakepublishing.com

Consultant: Marla Conn, ReadAbility, Inc.
Editorial direction and book production: Red Line Editorial

Photo Credits: Kali Nine LLC/iStockphoto, cover, 1; digitalskillet/
iStockphoto, 4; Viktor Gladkov/Shutterstock Images, 6; Dejan Ristovski/
iStock/Thinkstock, 8; RuslanDashinsky/iStockphoto, 10; Dennis
Tokarzewski/Hemera/Thinkstock, 12; Shutterstock Images, 14; Sura
Nualpradid/Shutterstock Images, 16; MaszaS/Shutterstock Images, 18;
Bonita R. Cheshier/Shutterstock Images, 20

Library of Congress Cataloging-in-Publication Data
Felix, Rebecca, 1984-
  Visiting the beach in summer / by Rebecca Felix.
    pages cm.
  Includes index.
  ISBN 978-1-63137-598-9 (hardcover) -- ISBN 978-1-63137-643-6 (pbk.)
-- ISBN 978-1-63137-688-7 (pdf ebook) -- ISBN 978-1-63137-733-4 (hosted
ebook)
  1. Beaches--Juvenile literature. 2. Summer--Juvenile literature. I. Title.

GB453.F45 2014
551.45›7--dc23
                                                        2014004449

Ch   owledge the work of The
                                   w.p21.org for more

TABLE OF CONTENTS

The Beach

Summer is hot. People spend time outside. Many visit the beach.

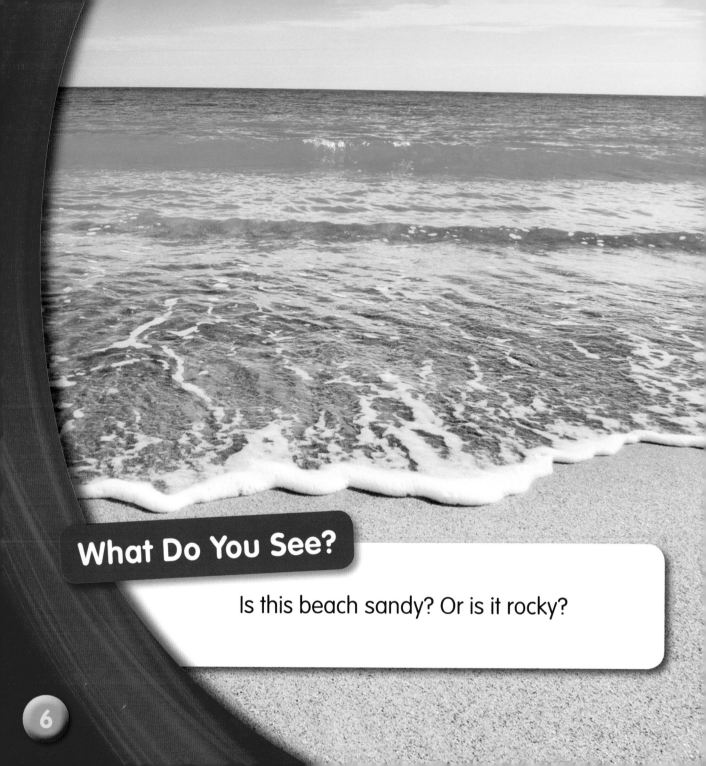

What Do You See?

Is this beach sandy? Or is it rocky?

A beach touches a lake or ocean. Sand or rocks cover it.

Sun

People enjoy sun at the beach. They wear **sunblock** to do so safely.

What is on Jo's head?

10

Fun

People have fun at the beach.
Jo plays with a beach ball.

Cal looks for crabs. He sees seagulls, too.

What Do You See?

Do you see the shells?

14

Rae finds shells. She builds sandcastles.

Water

Eli floats. He feels the **motion** of strong waves.

Ty and Matt swim. They **snorkel**.